BREAKING
CURSES

Identifying and Destroying Common Curses

Ryan LeStrange

TABLE OF CONTENTS

1

MY EXPERIENCE WITH A WORD CURSE

I was sitting in a church in California when I heard the Lord speak to me and say: "I have called you." I will never forget that moment. It was so vivid. I began to pray about what was next. I knew that I did not have the skills or knowledge to properly function in my ministry call, so I went into a season of prayer. The Lord directed my steps to move across the country and attend a spirit-filled Bible college. Going off to Bible college was a major step of faith. I was literally giving up everything that was familiar and launching out into the unknown.

As I was in my final stages of preparation to leave, I had an encounter that would greatly affect me. A relative of mine, who I esteemed greatly, began to tell me that I was missing the Lord. He boldly announced that I was not called to ministry and that this was a wrong decision. He told me that it would not work out and that I would fail. As you are reading this, I know it sounds mean-spirited, but I do not believe that was his intention. I believe he was very sad that I was leaving and was not properly processing his emotions. Having said that, it doesn't change the reality that his statements were a word curse.

The words went deep into my soul. They were powerful and drove a wedge into my emotions. As I went off to Bible college, it was one of the most difficult seasons of my life. I was in a completely different culture. I was stretched financially, and I was in a process of deliverance, so the enemy was screaming at me. Some days it seemed as though the heaviness was closing in around me. Certainly, God had moved me there, but the enemy was fighting against me.

On a particularly difficult day, I found myself filled with doubt and wanting to quit. The devil was harassing me greatly. In that moment, the words of my relative were swirling in my head. I could not only hear his words, but I could feel the weight of them. Maybe I had missed it. What if I was not even in the will of God and this whole battle was for nothing? I was questioning all of my decisions.

Suddenly, I had a revelation. This was a curse! The reason I felt so heavy was because I was reeling under the power of a word curse. The moment I recognized this, I broke the curse and commanded those words to die. I told the enemy that he could not bind my mind. I commanded my emotions to line up with the Word of God.

> A fool's mouth is his destruction, and his
> lips are the snare of his soul.
> — Proverbs 18:7 (NKJV)

Our mouths are agents of power. When we speak the Word of the Lord, we release creative power. When we speak the plans and thoughts of the enemy, we release demonic power. Words access the realms of the spirit.

A word curse releases demonic intent and creates heaviness and destruction.

> How shall I curse, whom God hath not cursed? or how shall I defy, whom the LORD hath not defied?
> — Numbers 23:8 (KJV)

A person who is blessed by God walks in divine power. They enjoy the power of God in their life, creating blessings and open doors. The blessing of God is the difference-maker. It creates avenues of life and abundance that are beyond a natural gift or ability.

A curse creates a demonic vacuum that attempts to suck a person into darkness and defeat. The enemy is an illegal trespasser when he tries to mess with the people of God. He cannot curse a man or woman whom God has blessed. Therefore, he searches for a breach in the wall. He looks for a way in. He can enter through the words of another, a trauma, an oath, or a number of ways. Even when a person curses you as my relative cursed me, that is a gateway. It comes to open up a spiritual door. You have to discern it and break its power.

OUR POSITION IN CHRIST

For He rescued us from the domain of darkness, and transferred us to the kingdom of His beloved Son, in whom we have redemption, the forgiveness of sins.

— Colossians 1:13-14

We have been translated! The blood of Jesus transferred us from one place to another. We have been divinely relocated. The Lord moved us from one realm to another and from one dimension to another. The sacrifice of Jesus at Calvary totally paid our debts and transferred us from the domain (rulership and authority) of darkness, and brought us out into the marvelous power and rule of Jesus! We are now authorized kingdom citizens filled with the power of God to change the world.

And you were dead in your trespasses and sins, in which you formerly walked according to the course of this world, according to the prince of the power of the air, of the spirit that is now working in the sons of disobedience. Among them we too all formerly lived in the lusts of our flesh, indulging the desires of the flesh and of the mind, and were by nature children of wrath, even as the rest. But God, being rich in mercy, because of His great love with which He loved us, even when we were dead in our transgressions, made us alive together with Christ (by grace you have been saved), and raised us up with Him, and seated us with Him in the heavenly places in Christ Jesus, so that in the ages to come He might show the surpassing riches of His grace in kindness toward us in Christ Jesus.

— Ephesians 2:1-7

In verse six of this passage, the word *heavenly* is the Greek word *epouranios* meaning, celestial, in the heavenly sphere, the sphere of spiritual activities; divine, spiritual.[1] The word *places* in this passage is a word that means in, on, or among. It denotes a location. The picture is that we have been removed from the kingdom of darkness and brought into the place or space of the kingdom of God. This speaks

1 https://www.biblehub.com/greek/2032.htm

of a total relocation. The blood of Jesus brought us out of the grip and place of darkness in order to position us in the place and space of the glorious kingdom of our God.

It is vital to know and understand our position as new covenant believers. This realization empowers us for effective spiritual warfare. Breaking curses is an act of war. It is severing demonic ties and allegiances. It is slamming shut the entry points of the works of hell. We are not praying from a defeated or weakened place. We are waging war from a position of power. This realization is part of our spiritual war arsenal.

> Therefore if you have been raised up with Christ, keep seeking the things above, where Christ is, seated at the right hand of God. Set your mind on the things above, not on the things that are on earth. For you have died and your life is hidden with Christ in God.
>
> — Colossians 3:1-3

A made-up mind is a key ingredient of living above every curse. Demonic curses seek to torment and afflict the mind. By meditating in the Word of God and renewing our mind to new creation realities, we empower faith and annihilate fear. We shut down the voice of the enemy simply by thinking on the things above. We engage the mind of the Spirit and our new nature.

THE POWER OF WORD CURSES

What is a *word curse*? It is a demonic announcement that opens a realm of the spirit to enforce the plans of hell. A *curse* is a solemn utterance intended to invoke a supernatural power to inflict harm or punishment on someone or something.

Word curses release hell's agenda. Everything in the spirit realm is created and established by words.

> By faith we understand that the worlds were framed by the word of God, so that the things which are seen were not made of things which are visible.
> — Hebrews 11:3 (NKJV)

> So will My word be which goes forth
> from My mouth;
> It will not return to Me empty,

Without accomplishing what I desire,
And without succeeding in the matter
for which I sent it.

— Isaiah 55:11

God creates by words. The enemy establishes demonic powers and influence by words. Prophets and prophetic people release spiritual utterances to build, create, and establish.

So they rose early in the morning and went out into the Wilderness of Tekoa; and as they went out, Jehoshaphat stood and said, "Hear me, O Judah and you inhabitants of Jerusalem: Believe in the Lord your God, and you shall be established; believe His prophets, and you shall prosper."

— 2 Chronicles 20:20 (NKJV)

There are two types of word curses that believers will deal with. There are overt witchcraft word curses when a person is operating under the power of the enemy and knowingly curses you. This is often the case with people who are under the power of evil spirits through false spiritual practices such as witchcraft or other occult activities. They are willingly participating in the wicked plans of the enemy. When they speak curses, it is intentional.

The second type of word curse is a work of the flesh. This is when fleshly people speak out of hurt, anger, offense, or fear. They say something that attacks the mind of another and decrees an evil outcome. It is also a demonic instrument. It is not an intentional act, but one that is born out of ignorance. Most believers will encounter these types of word curses at one point or another in their lives.

> Now the works of the flesh are manifest, which are these; Adultery, fornication, uncleanness, lasciviousness, idolatry, witchcraft, hatred, variance, emulations, wrath, strife, seditions, heresies, envyings, murders, drunkenness, revellings, and such like: of the which I tell you before, as I have also told you in time past, that they which do such things shall not inherit the kingdom of God.
>
> — Galatians 5:19-21 (KJV)

Paul is teaching the Galatian church about the power of walking in the Spirit. He makes the point that all of these evil things can spring from the works of the flesh. There is a level of witchcraft that can be empowered by a fleshly lifestyle. The person is not necessarily practicing Satanic worship, but they are not walking with God in a meaningful way. Their flesh is empowering the wrong activity in their life. This is how fleshly word curses are empowered. People begin to speak what they think and feel in a way that binds other people. They are manifesting demonic mindsets and activities from a place of ignorance.

SPEAK & DECREE

"Thou shalt also decree a thing, and it shall be established unto thee: and the light shall shine upon thy ways."

— Job 22:28 (KJV)

Believers are granted a place of power to speak by faith and command storms to cease, mountains to move, and the power of God to flow. Speaking is an act of faith.

We believe; therefore, we speak. To *decree* is to legislate in the realm of the spirit. We stand upon the Word of God and decree what God says. When we do this, we release the power of God.

LIFE & DEATH

> Death and life are in the power of the tongue...
>
> — Proverbs 18:21 (NKJV)

Our tongues can release the life of God into a situation. We can decree what heaven says, and the substance of victory fills the atmosphere. Conversely, when we agree with the enemy and say what he says, the power of darkness shows up on the scene. Our mouths are powerful weapons.

> "...the tongue is a fire, a world of iniquity: so is the tongue among our members, that it defileth the whole body, and setteth on fire the course of nature; and it is set on fire of hell."
>
> — James 3:6 (KJV)

Now Ahab told Jezebel all that Elijah had done, and how he had killed all the prophets with the sword. Then Jezebel sent a messenger to Elijah, saying, "So may the gods do to me and even more, if I do not make your life as the life of one of them by tomorrow about this time." And he was afraid and arose and ran for his life and came to Beersheba, which belongs to Judah, and left his servant there. But he himself went a day's journey into the wilderness, and came and sat down under a juniper tree; and he requested for himself that he might die, and said, "It is enough; now, O Lord, take my life, for I am not better than my fathers."

— 1 Kings 19:1-4

After Elijah's great victory, he came under heavy attack. Jezebel sent a messenger to him to release an evil decree. As the messenger spoke, fear and depression gripped the emotional inner man of Elijah. He became so vexed that he got up and ran, empowered by the spirit of fear. He spent an entire day running for his life! He finally got to the juniper tree and sought solace. A juniper tree is also known as a broom tree. It provides shade, a sweet fragrance, and beautiful white blooms. This was a place where Elijah could retreat and take comfort in the wilderness.

He ran a great distance, nearly one hundred miles in a day! This was because the spirit of fear had gripped him. Word curses will release fear, heaviness, and depression. A word curse often takes a toll on a prophetic person because of their heightened spiritual sensitivity and their ability to see.

When this curse was being spoken over Elijah, I believe he saw the words. They were hitting him on all levels. He saw himself dying. He saw the attack. The enemy attacked him in the area of his gift. This is a battle that many prophets and prophetic people go through. They have to learn the power of faith and authority so that they can effectively break word curses and not succumb to them. A word curse is intended to bind you, but the authority and faith of God can deliver you. As you realize who you are in Christ Jesus and discern the curse, you can break free.

SCRIPTURES ON THE POWER OF WORDS

"Whoever guards his mouth and tongue keeps his soul from troubles."

— Proverbs 21:23 (NKJV)

"The mouth of a righteous man is a well of life..."

— Proverbs 10:11 (KJV)

". . . the mouth of the upright shall deliver them."

— Proverbs 12:6 (KJV)

"A man shall be satisfied with good by the fruit of his mouth..."

— Proverbs 12:14 (KJV)

"...the tongue of the wise is health."

— Proverbs 12:18 (KJV)

"He that keeps his mouth [from speaking evil] keeps his life."

— Proverbs 13:3 (JUB *emphasis mine*)

"...the lips of the wise shall preserve them."
— Proverbs 14:3 (NKJV)

"A wholesome tongue is a tree of life: but perverseness therein is a breach in the spirit."
— Proverbs 15:4 (KJV)

"A gentle tongue [with its healing power] is a tree of life, but willful contrariness in it breaks down the spirit."
— Proverbs 15:4 (AMPC)

"The tongue of the wise uses knowledge aright [in a right way]."
— Proverbs 15:2 (KJ2000 *emphasis mine*)

"The heart of the wise teaches his mouth, and adds learning to his lips."
— Proverbs 16:23 (NKJV)

"Pleasant words are as an honeycomb, sweet to the soul, and health to the bones."
— Proverbs 16:24 (KJV)

SUMMARY

Word curses are very real demonic traps. They bring heaviness, pain, confusion, and trap doors in the realm of the spirit. Prophets and prophetic people often feel and see them in high definition. A strong realization of spiritual authority and the power of God is necessary to effectively break these curses.

DECREE

I break every word curse that has been
spoken over me.

I break the power of negative words.

I break the power of decrees and
proclamations over my life that do not
align with the will of God.

I uproot and pull down every controlling
word, every contrary word, every word and
decree that does not align with my identity
and assignment,
in the name of Jesus.

I command spirits of heaviness to go.

I command spirits of confusion to go.

I command every spirit of manipulation
and witchcraft to be broken over my life,
in the name of Jesus.

I release the power of the blood of Jesus
over my life.

I am who God says I am.

I can do what God says I can do.

I have all that God says I should have.

I am redeemed, I am blessed, and I am free,
in the name of Jesus.

Amen.

2

THE CURSE OF THE ORPHAN

Jesus came to the earth to restore us to the Father. He came to rip down the walls between us and God. He came to position us back in the kingdom of God with full access to the Father.

> Therefore if anyone is in Christ, he is a new creature; the old things passed away; behold, new things have come. Now all these things are from God, who reconciled us to Himself

> through Christ and gave us the ministry of
> reconciliation, namely, that God was in
> Christ reconciling the world to Himself,
> not counting their trespasses against them,
> and He has committed to us the word of
> reconciliation.
>
> — 2 Corinthians 5:17-19

The heart of the Father was to have fellowship with us again. He wanted His family back. In our role as new creations, we are serving God as His sons and daughters, not as spiritual orphans. He has given us an inheritance and brought great reconciliation into our lives.

> He predestined us to adoption as sons
> through Jesus Christ to Himself, according to the kind intention of His will, to the
> praise of the glory of His grace, which He
> freely bestowed on us in the Beloved.
>
> — Ephesians 1:5-6

I am convinced that we live well beneath our means because of a lack of revelation of the Father's love and good plans for us. Time and again, I have seen my fellow Christians get angry when preachers preach on the love of God and His mercy. They would rather beat the saints up and contaminate their faith. The reality is that our faith surges to another level when we come into the revelation of the love of God and our identity in Him.

Many people are struggling with a curse of orphanhood. This can come through abandonment and rejection. This can come through a family lineage. This can come through mental attacks. Many times, people struggling with this have gone through some type of trauma that needs to be dealt with. This is one of the things I absolutely love about the prophetic anointing. Prophets can see into the realm of the spirit, call forth the roots of a thing, and bring it under the blood of Jesus so that deliverance can take place.

Let me settle this in your mind! God never called you to be an orphan. You are not abandoned by God or neglected by Him. He has a good plan for you as your Father. He has already invited you to a place of wholeness. It may be a journey, but you can live totally free from the curse of orphanhood.

I will never forget a supernatural experience that I had in this area. I was traveling to go preach for a very good friend of mine. I was in an unusual season in which God had given me a mandate to preach and teach on impartation and the laying on of hands to everyone. It was a grueling but rewarding time. This assignment came through an encounter with an older minister who served as a general and father to many. He was pouring all that he had left into the next generation before he went on to his reward. His ministry has powerfully impacted me, and during this time, God took me to another level in impartation. I saw such profound miracles and breakthroughs as I poured out.

I arrived at my friend's church and could sense the atmosphere of hunger. I preached on impartation and told stories to build the faith of the people. The expectation in the room was palpable. I began to lay hands on every single person one at a time. A middle-aged man came through the line, and the moment he stood in front of me, I saw a curse trying to hold on to him. It was the curse of the orphan. I could see rejection and abandonment in the spirit.

As I asked the Lord for instruction, He reminded me of something so powerful. He told me to do the exact opposite of the curse. I began to speak over his life, breaking rejection and pain, but then the Lord told me to lay my right hand on him and release a blessing! Fathers bless.

Fathers impart. Fathers mantle, and fathers help to identify spiritual gifts and callings. I called him a mighty man and began to bless every area of his life that I had discerned the enemy trying to curse. The power of God hit this man and he crumpled to the floor like a wet rag, weeping. God was reaching down and breaking the bondage of that curse. The authority and anointing of God was totally destroying all bondage and shame. It was being broken into tiny pieces, one by one.

That day, the anointing and glory of God set the man free. I realized that I was on assignment to minister to him. This is one of the shifts we must make. We must realize that fathers come to confirm identity. They can break the lies of the enemy by releasing an apostolic blessing.

EFFECTS OF THE ORPHAN CURSE

The orphan curse opens the door for many evil spiritual influences. It creates a toxic mindset filled with wounded thoughts. Some of the effects of this demonic curse are:

1. Rejection

Orphans battle with rejection and can lash out. They also need an unhealthy amount of affirmation.

2. Pride & Leviathan

Leviathan is rooted in pride. Broken people often build strong walls to protect their pain and hide it. They can engage in extremely reckless and prideful behavior.

3. Fear & Intimidation

In the absence of the awareness of the Father's love and absolute acceptance, fear arises. This causes intimidation and limits the release of God-ordained exploits.

4. Lack of Glory & Ichabod

Rejected people can become wells without water. I have seen ministers who just didn't have the glory of God because they were not fully dwelling in the Father. They were living outside of sonship.

In church and ministry life, people battling an orphan curse can be difficult to work with. The enemy will pull at them and attempt to uproot them from God-ordained assignments and relationships.

They are unnecessarily defensive (because they have been self-providers and self-protectors). They can become very opportunistic, bouncing from alignment to alignment, searching for the best door or platform. They tend to view relationships as opportunities and don't do well with long-term commitments. They deem godly accountability and order as control. They vehemently resist any form of leadership that requires real submission. They will submit in name only to have an opportunity, but there is a continual seed of rebellion in their heart.

If they are prophetic in any way, they can easily engage in a form of prophetic ministry that overemphasizes correction without a spirit of love. They enjoy controversy and the strife that it causes. They are typically drawn to other prophetic voices of independence and those carrying an orphan heart.

They view ministry as an opportunity, not as family or a relationship. They quickly exit a ministry where enduring commitment is modeled and required. They are drawn to teaching that justifies a lone ranger theology. They spend more time blasting than building and identify problems instead of solutions.

God has a healing recipe for people battling this curse. They must be bold enough to confront the wounds in their heart and recognize the orphan spirit operating through them. They need to go deep inside and sow the Word and truth in their mind and spirit concerning adoption and acceptance. They have to build a new thought process about their identity in God. They must also tap into the power of God to heal their heart and set them free.

When confronting an orphan curse, believe God to send you to a valid and loving spiritual father who carries a heart like David. You do not want a Saul who is equally broken and will dominate you. When God leads you to a true leader, dive deep and trust Him. The relationship will uncover hidden wounds over time, and you may experience some emotional upheaval, but just stand and refuse to give up! This type of relationship is a vital part of your healing process.

SUMMARY

Your entry into the kingdom of God was accomplished through the shed blood of Jesus Christ. He paid the price to bring you into the family of God. This reality will override and abort the plans of the enemy. If you have the mindset of an orphan, you must renew your mind. You must get into the Word of God to find out who God says you are. There is power in your salvation and redemption. You no longer have to self-protect, self-guide, and self-provide. You can rely on and trust the Father.

Your journey out of an orphan mindset may not be easy, but it is worth it! You will have to quickly recognize old behaviors and command them to stop. You will have to speak and meditate on the Word of God. Your journey will lead you straight into the heart of the Father where all freedom exists. You are adopted, forgiven, and accepted.

DECREE

Lord, I thank you that I am accepted in
the beloved.

You are my Father and I lack no good
thing.

I break every curse of abandonment
and shame off my life.

I decree that I am not an orphan.

I do not think like an orphan.

I do not live like an orphan.

I do not operate as an orphan.

I am your child and you are my Father.

I receive your love in my life.

I decree your goodness, kindness, love, and mercy over my life.

I receive your adoption and I break the spirit of fear off my life.

I rest in you. I trust you. I am complete in you.

I break every orphan curse. I break past abandonment and rejection, in the name of Jesus.

I release the power of the blood of Jesus over my life, in the mighty name of Jesus. Amen.

3

THE CURSE OF THE VAGABOND

This is a demonic curse that comes upon people to uproot them, steal their prosperity, and rob their fruitfulness. It usually enters the life of a person through family curses or trauma. Prophetic people can fall prey to this by embracing a false mentality that instability is prophetic. While prophets and prophetic people love new things, it is very important that they develop a healthy root system, strong relationships, and healthy theology.

> And in process of time it came to pass, that Cain brought of the fruit of the ground an offering unto the Lord. And Abel, he also brought of the firstlings of his flock and of the fat thereof. And the Lord had respect unto Abel and to his offering: But unto Cain and to his offering he had not respect. And Cain was very wroth, and his countenance fell. And the Lord said unto Cain, Why art thou wroth? and why is thy countenance fallen? If thou doest well, shalt thou not be accepted? and if thou doest not well, sin lieth at the door. And unto thee shall be his desire, and thou shalt rule over him. And Cain talked with Abel his brother: and it came to pass, when they were in the field, that Cain rose up against Abel his brother, and slew him. And the Lord said unto Cain, Where is Abel thy brother? And he said, I know not: Am I my brother's keeper? And

he said, What hast thou done? the voice of thy brother's blood crieth unto me from the ground. And now art thou cursed from the earth, which hath opened her mouth to receive thy brother's blood from thy hand; When thou tillest the ground, it shall not henceforth yield unto thee her strength; a fugitive and a vagabond shalt thou be in the earth.

— Genesis 4:3-12 (KJV)

Cain murdered his own brother in an act of rage. His anger boiled over to the point of committing the first murder in the Bible. As a result, Cain fell under the curse of the vagabond spirit! He was doomed to roam, to wander, to struggle, and to be defeated. This is the vagabond curse in action! To further understand the nature of this curse, let's look at some word definitions.

The word *vagabond* in the Bible has the meaning of fugitive; to wander (aimlessly), move to and fro, flee, disappear, to stroll, or wander about.[2]

2 http://www.kingjamesbibledictionary.com/StrongsNo/H5110/vagabond

In English, the word *vagabond* means a person who wanders from place to place without a fixed home: one leading a vagabond life, vagrant, wandering; leading an unsettled, irresponsible, or disreputable life: to wander in the manner of a vagabond: roam about.

The word *wander* means indifferent. No set course, no navigation of destiny. To *roam* means moving from place to place, aimlessly journeying. The picture is of a person bound by a demonic curse without a home, without a healthy foundation, roaming without aim or direction. This is one way that the enemy gets into the lives of prophetic people. He convinces them that continual change in direction, without godly wisdom, counsel, and longevity, is God's plan. He steals their money by getting them out ahead of the plan of God. He steals their energy by constantly moving them from place to place without results. Eventually, they become disillusioned and falsely believe it is God's fault.

A vagabond doesn't welcome oversight or correction. A vagabond shuns the voice of wisdom. Many times, a vagabond can prophesy and receive revelation, but they are relationally and emotionally unhealthy. They will come into a ministry and make a lot of promises, only to uproot and leave the leaders disappointed before God releases them. In fact, they are continually looking for the release instead of investing in long-term, strategic plans and relationships.

Vagabonds find a way to spiritualize their lack of roots. They disguise instability and brokenness in hyper-spiritual language. Vagabonds roam from place to place without covenant connections.

Vagabonds do not confront hurts to receive healing from past wounds. This is usually the way the curse gained a foothold. There are times when vagabonds may have received an evil impartation from an unstable leader. When this happens, it must be broken off and the power of deliverance administered to break every cord.

SUMMARY

A vagabond curse blocks the revelation of the Father's love and creates a nomadic identity. If you lack commitment and long-term fruit, this may be the root cause. It can be a great challenge to confront this issue and decide to be planted, but it is the place of planting that produces fruit. Creating strong, healthy spiritual relationships and commitments will help solidify your freedom.

DECREE

I break every roaming spirit off my life,
in the name of Jesus.

I decree that I am not a spiritual nomad.

I move in the purposes and timing of God.

I move in the direction of the Holy Spirit.

I am led, guided, and directed to fruit-
bearing assignments and activities.

I am stable, consistent, and solid.

I command rejection to go.

I command deception to go.

I command fear of commitment to go.

I break the vagabond curse off my life,
in the name of Jesus. Amen.

4

THE CURSES OF INFIRMITY & DISEASE

One operation of demonic power is curses that manifest in the physical body. There are times that unexplainable afflictions plague a person. They experience unusual battles with infirmity, sickness, pain, and affliction. They cannot seem to break free and receive the healing power of God.

> And there was a woman who for eighteen years had had a sickness caused by a spirit;

and she was bent double, and could not
straighten up at all. When Jesus saw her,
He called her over and said to her, "Woman,
you are freed from your sickness." And He
laid His hands on her; and immediately she
was made erect again and *began* glorifying
God.

— Luke 13:11-13

This woman had a sickness that was caused by a demon!
There was a demonic entity residing in the woman's body
wreaking havoc. When Jesus ministered to her and loosed
her from the infirmity, He broke the power of hell off her
physical body! He released the power of God to heal her
and set her free. In a moment, the bondage was broken.

How God anointed Jesus of Nazareth with
the Holy Ghost and with power: who went
about doing good, and healing all that were
oppressed of the devil; for God was with
him.

— Acts 10:38 (KJV)

Jesus did not separate the two. He healed and set free at the same time. I believe that sickness is a work of the enemy sent to destroy the overall well-being of a believer. Many times when people are under some type of spiritual attack, they begin to battle physical symptoms.

I do not believe that we have clear guidance to conclude that all sickness is caused by a particular spirit. I believe that natural laws can affect our physical bodies. This is where the ministry of healing can be so powerful. God can break the effects of a physical challenge and release His power.

> Insomuch that they brought forth the sick into the streets, and laid them on beds and couches, that at the least the shadow of Peter passing by might overshadow some of them. There came also a multitude out of the cities round about unto Jerusalem, bringing sick folks, and them which were vexed with unclean spirits: and they were healed every one.
>
> — Acts 5:15-16 (KJV)

The early church had power that brought about healing and deliverance. All too often today, we see these two mighty flows of heaven separated, but in the early church they worked together. People received deliverance, demons were cast out, and the anointing of God flowed to heal bodies. Revival was a big wild outpouring of the Spirit of God. Heaven touched down on earth.

SUMMARY

A curse of infirmity comes to disrupt the plan of God in your life by bringing sickness and disease. It comes to rob you of your time, your energy, and your resources. It comes to isolate and frustrate you.

One of the powerful ministries of Jesus is healing. He paid the price for you to walk in divine health. You can believe Him for your healing and miracle. You can also pluck up every demonic root system that is empowering sickness and disease in your life. Your faith can tap the power of God for miracles and healing.

DECREE

I command sickness and disease
to go from my body now,
in the name of Jesus.

I thank you, Lord, that you sent your word
to heal my disease.

I receive your healing power now.

I activate my faith to receive
your mighty power.

I break all curses of infirmity
that would come against me.

I say that my body is healed and whole.

I say that your life is flowing through me.

I command every cell,
every muscle, every organ,
every tissue, and every gland to be healed,
in the name of Jesus.

I say that I am the healed of the Lord.

I say that I walk in health,
in the name of Jesus.

I claim my healing and miracle now,
in the name of Jesus. Amen.

5

FAMILY CURSES & FAMILY BLESSINGS

We must begin with the understanding that blessings are in the bloodline. God causes families that make covenant with Him to be blessed. The obedience of the family leaders passes down. It was always God's plan to use and bless families!

> "As for me, this is my covenant with them,"
> says the Lord. "My Spirit, who is on you,

will not depart from you, and my words
that I have put in your mouth will always
be on your lips, on the lips of your children
and on the lips of their descendants—from
this time on and forever," says the Lord.

— Isaiah 59:21 (NIV)

For I will pour water on the thirsty land,
and streams on the dry ground;
I will pour out my Spirit on your offspring,
and my blessing on your descendants.
They will spring up like grass in a meadow,
like poplar trees by flowing streams.

— Isaiah 44:3-4 (NIV)

The righteous lead blameless lives;
blessed are their children after them.

— Proverbs 20:7 (NIV)

The Spirit of the Lord works in families. He pours
Himself out upon the generations! You practice obedience in order to get the blessing for your children and your

children's children. This is a part of God's nature. He keeps covenant with His people.

There is a generational inheritance with your family name on it! However, blessings are not the only form of spiritual inheritance that can be passed down generationally. Curses can be passed down too. The enemy will attempt to place demonic plans and spirits in the bloodline.

> You shall not worship them or serve them;
> for I, the Lord your God, am a jealous God,
> visiting the iniquity of the fathers on the
> children, on the third and the fourth gener-
> ations of those who hate Me.
>
> — Exodus 20:5

This Old Testament warning was speaking of the long-term effects of generational curses. The idolatry and wickedness of the parent would be passed down for several generations. This is the work of the enemy in family bloodlines. The enemy comes to steal and rob a family by getting one generation to open doors that affect another generation.

'You shall not make for yourself an idol, *or* any likeness *of* what is in heaven above or on the earth beneath or in the water under the earth. You shall not worship them or serve them; for I, the Lord your God, am a jealous God, visiting the iniquity of the fathers on the children, and on the third and the fourth *generations* of those who hate Me.

— Deuteronomy 5:8-9

We see the same principles in these verses in Deuteronomy. There is fierce debate about generational curses, and at various times, I have been on either side of the debate as my thinking has evolved. I readily admit that the above scriptures are Old Testament, which basically means they are B.C.—before Christ. So as a believer, we are born into a new and better way. We have royal blood and the DNA of heaven. The argument, then, is that we are not under a curse, and I actually agree, but with a warning. You see, your family and bloodline may have been involved in things that opened doors for bloodline curses and familiar spirits.

I saw a terrible issue in a family with a spirit of insanity. It manifested in multiple generations and effectively robbed people of healthy lives. In one instance, a man had lost his mind and was being tormented by evil spirits. You could command the demons to be silent and the man would stop speaking. The problem was he would never fully submit to Jesus and receive any type of deliverance.

Later, he was out partying with a young relative when he suddenly died. The young man with him immediately began to manifest the same behaviors, attitudes, and even facial expressions. That demon was familiar with that bloodline and jumped from one family member to the next. It was clearly a generational curse in operation.

The reality is that demons get in families and bloodlines. Curses take place. It is critical that we form a theology about our new nature that allows us to tap into the plan of God for our lives and break every curse. Once we have identified a demonic root system in our family, we must then bind it, break it, and release the power of the blood of Jesus.

We then have to tap into the reality of born-again living. To be *born again* means that I have a brand new nature. Colossians 3:9-10 states, "Lie not one to another, seeing that ye have put off the old man with his deeds; And have put on the new man, which is renewed in knowledge after the image of him that created him" (KJV).

Walking in the Spirit empowers you to walk in the new nature. As you progressively journey deeper into the ways of God, you break the chains of the curse and manifest your God-DNA. To be clear, it is not just a decision, but a daily surrender and yielding to the Lord as you walk with Him. You spend time in His Word, you renew your mind, and you worship God. Then you pray in the Spirit and allow the perfect prayer to flow through you. It bypasses your human intellect and understanding in order to establish the Word of God and the will of God in your life.

> There is therefore now no condemnation to
> them which are in Christ Jesus, who walk
> not after the flesh, but after the Spirit.
> — Romans 8:1 (KJV)

There is a school of thought among some theologians and believers that does not recognize curses or the ministry of deliverance. Part of the disagreement seems to be centered around the idea that deliverance removes personal responsibility. Yet, on the other side of deliverance is an enforcement plan. That plan consists of my daily walk with God and purposeful engagement in the realm of the spirit according to His Word. This requires discipline. As I build up my spirit man and yield to God, I put the dictates of the flesh and its old appetites to death.

> For if ye live after the flesh, ye shall die: but if ye through the Spirit do mortify the deeds of the body, ye shall live. For as many as are led by the Spirit of God, they are the sons of God.
>
> — Romans 8:13-14 (KJV)

The word *mortify* here is the origin of the word *mortician*. The Holy Spirit has a mandate in your life. One of His jobs is to lead you to the place of death in the flesh and fleshly desires so that you can live in the Spirit and fulfill godly desires. Your new nature and the nature of God reveal ultimate and lasting freedom. As you come into full understanding of the grace and power of God in your life, you walk free from every bloodline curse. It is a relational journey empowered by the Spirit of God.

By boldly claiming your rights in Christ Jesus and appropriating the blood of the Lamb, you can break the cords of generational curses and activate your new nature. Confess and decree that you live out of your spirit and walk in the newness of God. Realize that there is absolutely no curse contained in your new nature!

SUMMARY

God has a plan for your family. He has generational callings and blessings. He has provision and assignments for families. He is a covenant-keeping God. Satan also looks for open doors and footholds. It is important to recognize certain patterns of bondage in your family and use your faith to break every attack and curse. You are a bloodline curse-breaker! You are granted the power of God to destroy the power of darkness over your family.

DECREE

I command every generational curse over my life
and associated with my family to be broken off
of me, in the name of Jesus.

I decree that the shed blood
of Jesus makes me free.

I decree that the power of God delivers me.

I decree that I am a new creation.

I destroy every work of iniquity
that would try to operate in my life.

I destroy the effects of the sins
of my relatives on my life, by the power of God.

I decree that I am a new creation;
old things are passed away, and I am brand new.

I am new through the blood of the Lamb
of God. The power of God is renewing and
restoring me. The glory of God is surrounding
and filling me.

I break and destroy all generational curses over
my life, in the name of Jesus. Amen.

(If you know of particular spiritual issues in your
bloodline, make sure you call them out. Repent
of them and break them off your life. If you
know the enemy is buffeting you through family
curses, but are not sure what they are, ask Holy
Spirit for direction. He can illuminate
your understanding.)

6

COMMON ACTIONS THAT PRODUCE CURSES

Scripture is very clear that certain actions produce certain reactions; certain seeds produce certain harvests. The wisdom books of the Bible confirm this. Demons enter the life of a person through doors, windows, and legal breaches in the spirit. One of the most powerful acts of deliverance is discerning the act or door that has been opened, repenting of it, and then slamming it shut.

Like the sparrow in her wandering, like the
swallow in her flying,
So the curse without cause does not come
and alight [on the undeserving].

— Proverbs 26:2 (AMP)

He who digs a pit [for others] may fall into
it, and a serpent may bite him who breaks
through a [stone] wall.

— Ecclesiastes 10:8 (AMP)

Curses do not randomly come into our lives. Either
something we have done, or something someone in our
bloodline has done, introduced it. And the cause of a curse
is also sin. The enemy uses these breaches to introduce a
curse.

The Bible says there are three main categories of sin we
can encounter in this world.

For all that is in the world—the lust of the
flesh, the lust of the eyes, and the pride of

life—is not of the Father but is of the world.
— 1 John 2:16 (NKJV)

We have already discussed some prominent curses in this book. Now I'd like to share with you some other common actions that have the ability to initiate curses in the life of an individual or in a bloodline.

1. ADDICTION

Any action that is compulsive and tormenting to your spirit. The action itself may not be sinful (e.g. eating), yet if it becomes something you cannot control, it has become toxic and demonic.

1. Gluttony
2. Nicotine
3. Alcoholism
4. Drugs (prescription and illegal)
5. Masturbation, Pornography, & Sex
6. Cuttings in the Flesh (emotional cutting, tattoos, piercings, plastic surgery)

2. SEXUAL IMMORALITY & PERVERSION

Any sexual act that breaks the boundaries of the biblical marriage covenant or transgresses the parameters of Scripture.

1. Lust
2. Masturbation
3. Pornography
4. Fornication
5. Adultery
6. Homosexuality/Lesbianism
7. Bisexuality
8. Polygamy & Polyandry
9. Threesomes & Throuples
10. Polyamory
11. Incest
12. Bestiality/Zoophilia

3. ILLEGAL GAIN

Any unethical, illegal, immoral, or evil means by which money or material items are gained.

1. Covetousness
2. Avarice
3. Theft
4. Embezzlement

5. Extortion
6. Corruption (i.e. in business or government)
7. Systemic Racism
8. Slavery (i.e. Transatlantic slavetrade, sex trafficking, human trafficking, etc.)

4. WITCHCRAFT

Any form of manipulation, intimidation, or domination.

1. Rebellion
2. Sorcery
3. Divination
4. False Prophecy (prophecy with ulterior motives or from an unclean spirit)
5. Verbal Assaults
6. Gossip

5. IDOLATRY

Praying to or worshiping anything that is not the God of the Bible, especially with the use of statues, images, and related objects. Also, any type of worship or ideology that a person elevates to the level of or above God and His Word.

1. Stubbornness
2. False Religion
3. Idolatry (the use of literal idols)

6. VIOLENCE

Any thoughts or acts of violence toward another creature or human being.

1. Envy & Jealousy
2. Rage & Wrath
3. Character Assassination
4. Physical Domination (i.e. domestic abuse, sexual abuse, animal abuse, etc.)
5. Abortion & Murder

This is not an exhaustive list; however, it can serve as a helpful guideline. Just because someone participates in one of these sins does not mean that they will automatically come under a curse. It just means that the more you actively participate in it, the higher the likelihood that a curse can be introduced into your life and your bloodline.

Below are some additional scriptures that speak to what can produce a curse in the life of an individual or a bloodline.

> Do you not know that the unrighteous will not inherit the kingdom of God? Do not be deceived. Neither fornicators, nor idolaters, nor adulterers, nor homosexuals, nor

sodomites, nor thieves, nor covetous, nor drunkards, nor revilers, nor extortioners will inherit the kingdom of God.

— 1 Corinthians 6:9-10 (NKJV)

But it shall come to pass, if you do not obey the voice of the Lord your God, to observe carefully all His commandments and His statutes which I command you today, that all these curses will come upon you and overtake you.

— Deuteronomy 28:15 (NKJV)

Galatians 5:16-18 admonishes the believer to walk in the Spirit so you do not give into your carnal desires. Walking in the Spirit frees us from the penalty of the law, and places us in right standing with God. Then, in the next paragraph, it goes on to list the works of the flesh.

Now the works of the flesh are evident, which are: adultery, fornication, unclean-ness, lewdness, idolatry, sorcery, hatred,

> contentions, jealousies, outbursts of wrath, selfish ambitions, dissensions, heresies, envy, murders, drunkenness, revelries, and the like; of which I tell you beforehand, just as I also told you in time past, that those who practice such things will not inherit the kingdom of God.
>
> — Galatians 5:19-21 (NKJV)

Next, the apostle Paul teaches us what actions are righteous and identifies us as those who live and walk in the Spirit of God.

> But the fruit of the Spirit is love, joy, peace, longsuffering, kindness, goodness, faithfulness, gentleness, self-control. Against such there is no law. And those who are Christ's have crucified the flesh with its passions and desires. If we live in the Spirit, let us also walk in the Spirit. Let us not become conceited, provoking one another, envying one another.
>
> — Galatians 5:22-26 (NKJV)

We can't get around the fact that sin produces destruction. James said, "But each one is tempted when he is drawn away by his own desires and enticed. Then, when desire has conceived, it gives birth to sin; and sin, when it is full-grown, brings forth death" (James 1:14-15, NKJV).

Iniquity has the ability to produce a curse that can be passed down to our children and their children and for as long as someone in the bloodline chooses to perpetuate it. Iniquity is making a conscious choice to do what is wrong. The Hebrew word for iniquity is *avon*[3], which means crookedness, perverseness, or evil regarded as that which is not straight or upright; moral distortion.

We can make a conscious decision to sin; however, as believers, we can also make a decision not to sin and lead a life that glorifies God. This will produce the blessings of the Lord in our life and in the lives of our children and our children's children.

> For the law of the Spirit of life in Christ
> Jesus has made me free from the law of sin
> and death.
>
> — Romans 8:2 (NKJV)

3 https://www.biblestudytools.com/lexicons/hebrew/kjv/avon.html

SUMMARY

No curse can come into the life of an individual without it being initiated. Curses can be passed down generationally. Sin is the cause of these curses. Many sinful actions can produce a curse, although that does not mean a curse is automatic. Iniquity is a choice just as righteousness is a choice. We are called to walk in the Spirit and not fulfill the lusts of the flesh. This is how the blessing of the Lord is produced in our lives and in the lives of our descendants.

Walking in the Spirit can create an access point to the power of God. As we learn to live and walk in our new nature, we walk progressively out of the cords of sin and bondage. We overcome and walk in the blessings of God. The power of God is released as we move in our new nature and live from a place of authority and redemption. Freedom is the portion of sons! It is an inheritance blessing.

PRAYER

Lord, I repent of every sin I have committed that has produced a curse in my life. I also repent on behalf of those in my family, past and present, who have participated in sins that produced a curse in my life and in the lives of our descendants. I renounce every agreement I have with sin, iniquity, and the curse of hell in my life and my bloodline, in Jesus' name. Amen.

(Call out any particular sins in your bloodline of which you are aware. For anything else, ask Holy Spirit to lead you. Repent and renounce your agreement with them out loud.)

DECREE

I decree that I am a child of God and that
I walk according to the Spirit of God.

He leads me and guides me
in the paths of righteousness.

Sin and iniquity are not my portion.
Curses are not my portion.

I decree that I will not make any openings
in the spirit that allow the enemy to
infiltrate and attack my life. I build up
every hedge around my family and myself,
in the name of Jesus.

I decree that the law of the Spirit of Christ
sets me free from the law of sin and death.

I decree that I have
eternal life in Christ Jesus.

I walk in righteousness and I remain
in right standing with heaven.

The blessing of the Lord adds to me and
there is no sorrow in it.

I decree that the blessing of the Lord is on
my children, on their children, and on my
descendants for a thousand generations, in
the name of Jesus. Amen!

7

FIVE POWER WEAPONS TO BREAK WORD CURSES

As a believer, you have been granted authority over the power of the enemy. You can break all curses off your life. You can reverse word curses. You can break generational curses. The enemy uses word curses to invoke evil spiritual forces. Words are keys that open doors to the spirit realm. Many times we face spiritual warfare from things that have been declared over us and even things that we have declared. Once we recognize a word curse, we need to break it. Here are five weapons of warfare:

1. RENOUNCE

The word *renounce* means to give up, refuse, or resign usually by formal declaration. When you recognize a word curse, you break it and renounce it by your declaration! You then place a blessing where there was a curse. You begin to release the blessing over the area(s) of your life where the enemy had someone release a word curse. You align your tongue with the promises of God over your life.

The Lord spoke to Moses and told the priests to speak to them and bless them.

> Then the Lord spoke to Moses, saying,
> "Speak to Aaron and to his sons, saying,
> 'Thus you shall bless the sons of Israel. You
> shall say to them:
> The Lord bless you, and keep you;
> The Lord make His face shine on you,
> And be gracious to you;
> The Lord lift up His countenance on you,
> And give you peace.'"
>
> — Numbers 6:22-26

2. USE AUTHORITY

As a child of God, you have been granted legal authority over the power of the enemy. You have been placed in Christ above the power of the enemy. This means that you can decree, bind, loose, and command! The camp of the enemy has to obey the believer who knows their position of authority. So you do not ask, but you command!

> And what is the surpassing greatness of His power toward us who believe. These are in accordance with the working of the strength of His might which He brought about in Christ, when He raised Him from the dead and seated Him at His right hand in the heavenly places, far above all rule and authority and power and dominion, and every name that is named, not only in this age but also in the one to come. And He put all things in subjection under His feet, and gave Him as head over all things to the church, which is His body, the fullness of Him who fills all in all.
>
> — Ephesians 1:19-23

3. RELEASE THE POWER OF THE BLOOD

The blood of Jesus purchased your freedom. The blood is a powerful offensive weapon that pushes back the powers of the enemy. We can exercise the power of Jesus' blood and appropriate freedom.

> And they overcame him because of the blood of the Lamb and because of the word of their testimony, and they did not love their life even when faced with death.
>
> — Revelation 12:11

4. WALK BY FAITH

Faith aligns itself with the Word of God. It claims the Word as supreme truth and then takes action. Faith moves! Faith commands the mountains to move and declares the promise. Faith continues to focus on the promise no matter how many times the problem presents itself.

> For we walk by faith, not by sight.
>
> — 2 Corinthians 5:7 (KJV)

5. GET UNDER THE ANOINTING

The anointing destroys yokes! It removes the ties of bondage and releases life-changing freedom. Receiving the anointing of the Holy Spirit brings powerful freedom. A person coming out from under a word curse should get where the Holy Spirit is moving. Get hands laid upon them. Get under anointed worship. Create the atmosphere of heaven in their own house. The anointing undoes the weighty chains.

> And it shall come to pass in that day, that his burden shall be taken away from off thy shoulder, and his yoke from off thy neck, and the yoke shall be destroyed because of the anointing.
>
> — Isaiah 10:27 (KJV)

The power of God always trumps the power of the enemy! It is no contest. We do not study or teach on any type of demonic power to establish fear in the life of a believer, but to initiate effective spiritual warfare and deliverance strategies. I believe the Lord drew you to this writing to equip you to overcome every curse and walk in the blessings of God.

Jesus did not pay a partial price at Calvary! He gave it all so that you could live in the victory of God for your life. He brought you into a place of authority over the power of hell. You can terrorize and torment the devil. Your life can be a manifestation of the goodness and power of God. You can be an instrument of God's deliverance.

DECREE

I decree that I am coming
out of every attack.

I decree that I am strong and not weak.

I decree that I am filled
with power and glory.

I decree that my heart is
aligned with the Father.

No weapon formed against me prospers.
No demonic plan against me works.
No assault is effective.

I decree that I am covered,
protected, and empowered.

I am God's ambassador, and I go forth free
from all curses, in the majestic name of our
Lord Jesus Christ. Amen!

DECREES

ABANDONMENT

I break the spirit of abandonment off my life. I refuse to live with the mentality of an orphan! I am accepted in the beloved. I am loved. I am adopted and brought into the family of God through the complete work of Jesus at the cross. I am no longer afflicted or alone. I am free, loved, complete, and whole. I cast out every spirit of abandonment! I break your power and command you to go, in Jesus' name! Leave now and never return.

ADDICTION

I come against every spirit of addiction working in my life, in Jesus' name! I break ungodly desires and dependencies. I confess that I am an overcomer, in Jesus' name. I am not bound, because the blood of Jesus has made me free. My desires must line up with the Word of God. I break cycles of bondage, in Jesus' name. I break addictive cravings, in Jesus' name. I command my thought patterns to be normal and free from addiction. I command the chemistry of my body to be healed and whole, in Jesus' name. You foul spirit of addiction, I cast you out and command you to go from me now, in Jesus' name! I am no longer bound! I receive the miracle-working freedom of God Almighty in my mind, my body, and my life right now.

ABORTION & SUICIDE

I break shame and condemnation that is connected to the sin of abortion. I ask for and receive complete forgiveness for this sin. I break the hold of death over my life. I slam every door shut that was opened by this act. I shut the door to every abortive spirit coming against me. I shut the door to the spirit of barrenness. I shut the door to the spirit of shame. I shut the door to condemnation and guilt. I refuse to carry this weight any longer. You foul spirit of abortion, shame, and pain, I command you to go from me, in Jesus' name! I cast you and every spirit tied to you out, in the authority of Jesus' name. I boldly confess my freedom and full redemption. I am free now, in Jesus' name!

BARRENNESS

I confess that I am blessed! I am designed to multiply and be fruitful in every area of my life. I walk in the blessing of multiplication. My finances are fruitful. My mind is fruitful. My family is fruitful. My ministry is fruitful. My life is fruitful. I walk in the blessings of the God of Abraham. I break the spirit of barrenness off of my life! I command all barrenness to go from my mind, my emotions, my body, my money, my life, and my family, in Jesus' name.

CONFUSION

I have a sound mind! I am filled with the wisdom of God. I am led and directed by Holy Spirit. I clearly hear, know, and see. I discern the will of God. I am not confused. I break the spirit of confusion over my life, in Jesus' name! I command every spirit of confusion to leave me now.

DEATH

I am called to reflect the life of God! I am filled with God's nature and His life. I am free from the law of sin and death. I will live a long life. The Lord satisfies me with long life. I break every spirit of death and command it to go from me, in Jesus' name!

DEPRESSION (HEAVINESS)

I break the spirit of heaviness and depression, in Jesus' name! I am filled with joy. I am excited about life. I am full of energy. My mind and body are alert. Spirit of heaviness and depression go from me, in Jesus' name! No weapon formed against me shall prosper! I break every evil word curse off my life, in Jesus' name! I pull down false utterances and evil proclamations over my life. I release the blessings of heaven over me and my family. We are blessed and not cursed. We are free!

FAMILIAR SPIRITS

I break every familiar spirit off my life, in Jesus' name. I am not deceived. I am led by the Holy Ghost into all truth. I hear the voice of my Father. I am planted in the kingdom of God and I am not misled by demon powers. I cast familiar spirits out right now, in Jesus' name. I command your power to be broken over my life. I am delivered! I am free! Thank you, Jesus, I am free.

FEAR & PARANOIA

God has not given me a spirit of fear. He has given me a spirit of power, love, and a sound mind. I cast out the spirit of fear, every type of fear, and every symptom of fear, in Jesus' name. I command fear, anxiety, and paranoia to flee from my life now. Spirit of fear, go right now, in Jesus' name! I say that I am free of all fear. The good Shepherd heals my soul and my mind. I release your healing power over my emotions. I command stress, anxiety, fear, torment, paranoia, and every bit of anguish to go from me, in Jesus' name! I am not afraid! The Lord keeps me in perfect peace as my mind is stayed on Him, in Jesus' name!

IDOLATRY

I put no other gods before you, Lord. I repent for any area where I have worshipped anything or anyone but you, Lord. I surrender my life to you. I surrender my mind to you. I surrender my heart to you, Jesus. You are my Lord. I will have no other gods before you. I say that you are high and lifted up. You are the Exalted One, Lord. I cast idolatry out, in Jesus' name! I command you to go from me now. I break every idolatrous spirit off my life.

INFIRMITY

I break the spirit of infirmity off of my life. I confess that Jesus is my healer. I thank you, Lord, that I am loosed from the spirit of infirmity. I call forth the life of God in my body right now, in Jesus' name. I receive God's healing power and strength in every member of my body. Thank you, Jesus, that you are my miracle-worker and your mighty power is setting me free right now. I command every spirit of infirmity to go from me now, in Jesus' name!

INSANITY & SCHIZOPHRENIA

I have the mind of Christ. My thought patterns are normal. My mind is fixed on Jesus. My thoughts are aligned with the Word of God. I break the power of every spirit of insanity and mental instability. I release healing power over my mind. I bind all mental torment and harassment, in the name of Jesus. God is not the author of confusion, but the God of peace. I release God's authority over my emotions. I release God's blessing over my thinking. I cast out the spirit of insanity and double-mindedness, and I command you to go, in Jesus' name. I thank you, Lord, that I am normal. My mind is normal. My thoughts are normal. I am the healed of the Lord, in Jesus' name.

JEZEBEL & CONTROL

I break the lies, the intimidation, the domination, the manipulation, the seduction, and the oppression of Jezebel off of my life. I refuse to bow to the Jezebel spirit. I say that my mind is clear and my spirit alert. I am led by the Spirit of God. I am not dominated or controlled by any person or demon. I do not manipulate or control others. I say that I am confident in the power of my God. My mind is free from thoughts of control. I am strong and not weak, in Jesus' name. I am more than a conqueror. I break all the power of Jezebel off of my life. I command every plot, scheme, strategy, and assignment of Jezebel to be broken off my life, in Jesus' name!

POVERTY & LACK

Thank you, Lord, that you are my provider. You said that you take pleasure in the prosperity of your servant. I thank you, Lord, that I have more than enough. I declare that the mindset of poverty is broken off my life! I walk in abundance. There is no lack in my life. I am the head and not the tail. I lend and do not borrow. I break the power of lack over my life. I command lack to go from me, in Jesus' name!

PYTHON

I will not be constricted or restricted anymore. I renounce the python spirit, its lies, its squeeze, and its false prophecies over my life. I break the grip of python and command it to leave my life, in Jesus' name! I call forth a restoration of the wind of God in my life and the breath of heaven upon me.

RAGE, VIOLENCE & MURDER

I thank you, Lord, that I walk in the love and the peace of God. My mind, will, and emotions are aligned with your Word and your ways. I walk in love. I close every door in my life to anger, violence, and murder. I say that I am peaceful, I am patient, I am gentle, and I am kind, in Jesus' name. I do not commit acts of violence, and acts of violence are not committed against me. I command every spirit of rage, violence, and murder to go from me now, in Jesus' name!

RAPE & MOLESTATION

Thank you, Lord, for supernatural healing from every sexual violation over my life. You said that if anyone be in Christ, they are a new creation. I believe that you are making me brand new as if I was never violated. I thank you, Lord, for your healing and cleansing right now! I believe that your power is making me free. I am not tormented! I am not harassed! I am not ashamed! I am not afraid! I break the power of every spirit of sexual abuse, rape, and molestation right now, in Jesus' name! I command you to go from me now, in Jesus' name!

REBELLION

I break and bind every rebellious spirit, thought, and tendency in my life. I cast down vain imaginations and command my mind to line up with the Word of God. I love the Word and the ways of God. I am fully submitted to the will of my Father. Spirit of rebellion, you go from me now, in Jesus' name! I cast you out and command your power to be broken over my life.

REJECTION

I break rejection off of my life. I am not rejected by God. I am accepted by my Father. I am not a man-pleaser. I am delivered from the fear and approval of man. I am not easily offended. I do not get my feelings hurt easily. I am confident in God and who He has created me to be. I command the spirit of rejection to go from my life, in Jesus' name! I break rejection off every facet of my life. Go now. I am free!

RELIGIOUS SPIRIT

I refuse to operate in a religious spirit! I am a Jesus person, filled with the Holy Ghost, and on fire for God. I am not dry or stale. I am alive in the Spirit! I love the move of God. I embrace the move of God. I command every religious spirit to go from me, in Jesus' name! I command religious thought processes to go, in Jesus' name. I command religious attitudes to go, in Jesus' name. I command religious patterns to be broken, in Jesus' name.

SEXUAL SIN

You have made me to be pure before you. I command every spirit of sexual immorality and perversion to loose me, in the name of Jesus. I cast out perversion. Father, I ask you to create in me a clean heart, in the name of Jesus. My body is the temple of the Holy Ghost and I will not yield my members to sexual sin. I am not a slave to my flesh. My sexual desires line up with the Word of God, in Jesus' name. I confess that I have normal sexual appetites and desires. I thank you, Lord, for healing my mind and emotions. I break the shame attached to the lies of hell over my life in the area of sexual sin. My mind is free. My heart is free. My life is free, in Jesus' name. I am free!

SOUL TIES

Father, I thank you for absolute freedom. I come before you now and bring every ungodly soul tie before the throne of God. I ask for your healing power to come forth. You are restoring my soul. You are healing my mind, will, and emotions right now. I invite the healing power of Jesus on the scene.

Come, mighty Holy Spirit, and release your healing power. I break soul ties, in the name of Jesus. I command every yoke in my emotions to be broken off. I confess that I am free indeed!

TRAUMA

Thank you, Lord, for healing me from all trauma. I declare your healing power over emotional trauma. I declare your healing power over physical trauma. I declare your healing power over family and relationship trauma. I break the power of all trauma off of my life. I release your supernatural peace and healing power. I command the spirit of trauma to go from me, in Jesus' name! I speak shalom over every part of my life. God's supernatural peace is overtaking me. Nothing missing. Nothing lacking. Nothing broken. I am healed and whole, in Jesus' name.

ALL CURSES

I am blessed and not cursed. I am the head and not the tail. I am above and not beneath. I am blessed coming and going. Everywhere I go, I am blessed. I am chosen by God. I am loved by God. I am mantled by God. I am empowered by God. I break every curse off of my life, in Jesus' name! I break family curses. I break witchcraft curses. I break word curses. I command every curse to bow to the blood of Jesus! I break all curses over my life, in Jesus' name! Be broken now. I am free! I am blessed! I am redeemed!